Blessings from Above

A Deeper Look at the Beatitudes

Heather Hart

Blessings from Above
A Deeper Look at the Beatitudes

© 2014 by Heather Hart

Printed in the United States of America

ISBN: 978-1497477018

All rights reserved. No part of this publication may be reproduced, stored in a retrieval system, or transmitted by any means – electronic, mechanical, photographic (photocopying), recording, or otherwise – without prior permission in writing from the author, unless it is for the furtherance of the Gospel of salvation and given away free of charge.

All scripture quotations, unless otherwise indicated, are taken from the American Standard Version of the Bible which is in the public domain.

Scripture quotations marked "WNT" are taken from the Weymouth New Testament. The Weymouth New Testament was published in 1903 and is in the public domain.

Scripture quotations marked "KJV" are taken from the Holy Bible, King James Version, Cambridge, 1769.

Scripture quotations marked "WEB" are taken from the World English Bible® (WEB). The World English Bible is in the public domain and is not copyrighted.

Cover design by Paul and Heather Hart
Cover photo © seqoya - Fotolia.com

www.PaulandHeatherHart.com

Table of Contents

Introduction 7

Poor in Spirit..11

Those Who Mourn 15

The Meek 19

Hunger and Thirst..23

Merciful 27

Pure in Heart 31

Peacemakers...35

Persecuted 39

Conclusion..43

The Beatitudes

Blessed are the poor in spirit:
for theirs is the kingdom of heaven.

Blessed are they that mourn:
for they shall be comforted.

Blessed are the meek:
for they shall inherit the earth.

Blessed are they that hunger
and thirst after righteousness:
for they shall be filled.

Blessed are the merciful:
for they shall obtain mercy.

Blessed are the pure in heart:
for they shall see God.

Blessed are the peacemakers:
for they shall be called sons of God.

Blessed are they that have been persecuted for
righteousness' sake: for theirs is the kingdom of heaven.

Blessed are ye when men shall reproach you, and persecute
you, and say all manner of evil against you falsely,
for my sake.

Rejoice, and be exceeding glad:
for great is your reward in heaven:
for so persecuted they the prophets that were before you.

~ Matthew 5:3-12

Introduction

Blessings don't appear to be black and white. A well-paying job might seem like a blessing at first, but what if it keeps a father from his family? Is it still a blessing? For that matter, what really qualifies as a blessing?

Throughout this book, we are going to take a deeper look at what the Bible says are true blessings—or blessings from above. Specifically, we will be looking at Jesus' words in Matthew 5:1-12, which are commonly referred to as the beatitudes (also found in Luke 6:20-26.)

Just to give you a little bit of background, the beatitudes kick off the Sermon on the Mount. This sermon was a sort of orientation for the disciples. It contained the essence of all Christ's teaching. Throughout my study, I have seen it as Christ spelling out for His disciples exactly what to expect from following Him, and what He expected from them as people who represented Him—and the very first thing Jesus addressed was the attitude of their hearts.

It turns out, people back then weren't that different from us today—they wanted money and power. The Pharisees taught a prosperity gospel that said if you were truly blameless, then all would go well for you. If you were poor, on the other hand, God must be punishing you for your disobedience. If you tithed enough money, honored the priests, etc. you were good with God. But if you didn't give enough or didn't bow low enough, well... you must have sin issues that needed to be resolved (they got along great with Job's comforters).

Jesus wanted His disciples to know this was not His stance. He wanted them to know that following Him was not the path to fame and fortune, but one of suffering and humble living. Jesus didn't promise power and riches, but spoke of poverty and sorrow. Yet at the same time, Christ wanted them (and us) to know there is a reward for following Him—we will be truly blessed.

Now, before we get too far into this, it is important to note that blessed does not mean happy, and it certainly doesn't mean lucky. To be blessed by God means to experience hope and joy independent from our circumstances. It means we possess the favor of God. To be blessed is to be loved—to be cherished. True blessings come from love.

When God sent His Son, Jesus Christ, to die on the cross for our sins, we received His eternal favor. Through Christ and His teachings we will find everlasting peace, joy, love, forgiveness, and so much more. In other words, we will find true blessings when we let Christ into our lives.

As I went through this study, I asked myself three different questions:

1. How does what Jesus is teaching here differ from what the world teaches?

2. How should this affect my attitude—or what should it look like in my life?

Introduction

3. Do I have a superficial "Pharisee" faith in this area of my life, or a real, Christ-like faith rooted deeply in the person and Word of Christ?

I have done my best to cover the first two questions in each chapter of this book, but it is up to you to answer the third one on your own.

One thing I discovered early in this study was that the beatitudes are not multiple choice. We cannot pick which ones we want to claim and ignore the rest. They are a description of Christ's will for each of us, and these blessings are given to us when we accept Christ into our lives.

None of the beatitudes come from our own strength, but they are all things we are freely given through our Savior: humility, gentleness, a pure heart, the ability to show mercy... All of those attitudes come from Christ, and are cultivated in us by His Spirit.

While we go through this study, I hope each of us can look at ourselves to see if our attitudes reflect that which Christ has called us to, or that of the world.

I have really enjoyed digging into God's Word during the course of the last few months, and I hope God can use this book to open your eyes to the blessings in your life.

" O taste and see that the LORD is good: blessed is the man that trusteth in him."

~ Psalm 34:8 (KJV)

In Other Words...

Throughout this book, you will find sections like this one. These are here with the hope that you will take what the Bible says and put it into your own words. I have always found I retain things better when I am able to think it through on my own. So I'll provide you with questions and scriptures to look up to help you come up with biblical answers and solidify your understanding of what Jesus was teaching.

You will get the most out of this book if you don't stop with the words I have written, but take the time to look up the passages referenced in these sections and answer the questions honestly—search your heart and let God speak to you. My goal in writing Bible studies isn't just to tell you what God has been teaching me, it's to help you see what God's Word really says and grow in your relationship with Him.

You should also know that I am not some brilliant theologian, but I do learn from God's Word each time I open it—and you can, too. Hopefully these sections will help you walk away with a heart set on Christ and a deeper understanding of the blessings He's already given to you.

Here is a short example of what's to come:

- ❖ What does it mean to be "blessed"? (Look up: Luke 1:45; Romans 4:7-8; Galatians 3:8-9)

- ❖ When it comes to true blessings, do I have a superficial "Pharisee" faith, or a real, Christ-like faith rooted deeply in the person and Word of Christ? Take a moment to write, in your own words, what you believe about blessings.

Chapter One

Poor in Spirit

*"Blessed are the poor in spirit:
for theirs is the kingdom of heaven."*
~ Matthew 5:3

A few years back, I went through a wonderful study through the seven churches in the book of Revelation. That study has stayed with me over the years and I wanted to share part of it with you here.

One of the churches was the church of Laodicea (Revelation 3:14-22) and it was rich in the eyes of the world. The members of that church proclaimed their riches, yet Jesus said they were wretched, pitiful, poor, blind, and naked—and the worst part is they didn't even realize it. This was the lukewarm church that proclaimed Christ, but weren't dependent on Him.

The church in Laodicea was rebuked by Christ—and that rebuke was the first thing that came to mind when I read, *"Blessed are the poor in spirit..."* Isn't it funny how we often read a scripture and automatically think of someone who didn't or doesn't "get it"? That happens to me more often than I care to admit, but I know that in order to grow I have to think inward, not outward.

The first step towards thinking inward when it comes to this verse is simply to know what it means to be poor in spirit. I asked my ladies' Bible study group what they thought it meant to be poor in spirit and here are some of the things they said:

~ It's the opposite of me first.
~ To think of others before yourself.
~ To have a servant's heart.
~ To be absolutely destitute.
~ To be aware of sinfulness.
~ To be humble.
~ To be dependent on Christ.
~ To put Christ first.

Simply put, we are poor in spirit when we humble ourselves before God and acknowledge that we are sinners in need of a Savior. The church of Laodicea missed out on an amazing blessing by failing to humble themselves (and sometimes I do, too).

I think Jesus listed this as the first beatitude because without humbling ourselves before God—without knowing our need for Christ—all the other beatitudes are null and void. We will talk about this more throughout the coming chapters, but true blessings are dependent on knowing who God is and what He has done for us.

When we accept Christ as our Savior, God graciously gives us so much. He blesses us with eternal life, bestows His righteousness on us, fills us with His Spirit, and calls us His own. But how often do we forget that it all comes from Him? To constantly be poor in spirit we need to remember we are not capable of any of it on our own and acknowledge our need for Jesus is unending.

In his commentary of the book of Matthew, William Barclay said it this way: *"O the bliss of the man who has realized his own utter helplessness, and who has put his whole trust in God."*[1] In other words, to consistently be poor in spirit is to remember we are the worst of sinners and our need for Jesus is unending (1 Timothy 1:15-16). Which reminds me of another one of the churches mentioned in Revelation chapter 3, and that's the church in Philadelphia (found in verses 7-13).

The church in Philadelphia wasn't rich in any sense of the world. They were oppressed, beaten down, and had little strength—but they refused to deny Christ. With what little strength they had, they proclaimed His name, kept His Word, and endured patiently every trial that came their way.

And Jesus commended them.

Jesus promised that no one would ever take their crown. He said those who were causing their problems here on earth would one day acknowledge they were loved by God. Moreover, He promised them a place in the New Jerusalem and eternity with Christ—He promised them the kingdom of heaven.

The blessing for those who are poor in spirit is simply, yet magnificently, to know Christ as lord. It's not just the blessing of knowing what is to come, but to have the peace and joy God gives us when we surrender our lives to serve Him.

When Christ reigns in our hearts, we are members of His kingdom both now and for all eternity. And what a true blessing that is.

Blessings from Above

*"I will bless the LORD at all times:
his praise shall continually be in my mouth.
My soul shall make her boast in the LORD:
the humble shall hear thereof, and be glad.
O magnify the LORD with me,
and let us exalt his name together."*
~ Psalm 34:1-3 (KJV)

In Other Words...

- ❖ What does it mean to be poor in spirit? (James 2:5; Matthew 23:12; James 4:6-10)

- ❖ How does being poor in spirit effect our daily lives as Christians? (2 Corinthians 8:9; 1 Peter 5:6-7; Psalm 149:4; Psalm 40:17)

- ❖ What is the Kingdom of Heaven and how is it a blessing to those who are poor in spirit? (Luke 17:20-21; Romans 14:17)

- ❖ Do I have a superficial "Pharisee" faith in this area of my life, or a real Christ-like faith that is rooted deep in the person and Word of Christ? Take a moment to write out in your own words what you believe about this beatitude.

Chapter Two

Those Who Mourn

*"Blessed are they that mourn:
for they shall be comforted."*
~ Matthew 5:4

There is an Arab proverb that says, *"All sunshine makes a desert."* It means if it never rains, nothing can grow. I think the same is true when it comes to our hearts. Ecclesiastes says there is a time for everything and a season for every activity under the sun. That includes a time to weep and mourn and a time to laugh and dance (3:1-4).

I don't think you need me to tell you mourning isn't fun. All of us have mourned about someone or over something at one point in time or another. And, by the world's standards, there is nothing great about it.

Mourning is, however, an emotion created by God. God uses times of mourning to help us grow. To grow closer to Him. To grow our faith. To deepen our understanding of His love for us…

Laura Story has a beautiful song called "Blessings." In it she sings about how sometimes blessings come in the form of raindrops, and how tears can bring healing. In an interview she gave about the song she said, *"... there is a blessedness that comes through waiting on the Lord. There is an intimacy in our walk with the Lord that comes through walking through that valley. There is a reliance on His Word that we only know when everything else fades away. And in that sense, I truly feel like I am blessed."* [2]

Mourning can be a blessing by bringing us closer to Christ, but it's also the first step towards surrendering our lives to Christ. We have to mourn over our sin before we will turn to Christ—first when we accept Him as our Savoir, but then also with our troubles, failures, and feelings for the rest of our lives. And when we do turn to Him, God comforts us and can turn our mourning into joy—or fill us with His peace that surpasses all understanding.

As Christians, we know who God is, what He has done. We have the promise of an eternity yet to come. Because of those things we have hope, comfort and joy no matter what the circumstances, even in times of mourning and sorrow.

The book of Luke says it this way, *"Blessed are you who weep now, for you will laugh,"* (6:21) and *"Woe to you who laugh now, for you will mourn and weep."* (6:25)

One of the ladies I study with said, when it's worded that way, it's a good reminder of the ups and downs of life. Life might be good for you now, but sorrows will come. It's important to lean on Christ in the good times, so you have a firm foundation for mourning when it comes. But we also have to remember those who don't mourn over their sin, choosing to go through life without repenting, will suffer in eternity. They might not mourn now, but they will. And those of us who are painfully aware of our sin now, we will be able to rejoice and laugh with Christ when we get to Heaven.

I mentioned that mourning is a God-created emotion. One thing I'm learning is that true mourning is a side effect of love. Have you ever noticed you grieve more when a tragedy involves someone you know personally and love deeply? We recently had a friend of my husband's family die. I mourned for him (and I still do), but not to the same degree that his daughter or even my husband who loved him dearly. Love makes it different. The more you love, the more you mourn.

When we become Christians, God softens our hearts and fills us with His love. We are then saddened by sin and grieve with those around us because we are overflowing with love for them from Christ. And when we love others the way God created us to love, we mourn when they mourn and we mourn over their sin (whether they do or not).

Yet, as Christians, we also know where true comfort and eternal joy can be found. We aren't left with inconsolable tears, but we take our pain to the foot of the cross and let the God of all comfort replace our hurts with His peace. When we come to Him, He becomes our refuge and ever-present help in trouble (Psalm 46:1), and what a blessing that is.

"If there is therefore any exhortation in Christ,
if any consolation of love, if any fellowship of the Spirit,
if any tender mercies and compassion, make my joy full,
by being like-minded, having the same love,
being of one accord, of one mind;
doing nothing through rivalry or through conceit,

> *but in humility, each counting others better than himself;*
> *each of you not just looking to his own things,*
> *but each of you also to the things of others."*
> ~ Philippians 2:1-4 (WEB)

In Other Words…

- ❖ Have you thought about mourning as a God given emotion born out of love? How does that effect your view of mourning? (Ecclesiastes 7:3)

- ❖ How does God comfort believers when they mourn? (Psalm 119:49-56; 2 Corinthians 1:3-7; Revelation 21:1-4)

- ❖ Do I have a superficial "Pharisee" faith when it comes to mourning, or a real Christ-like faith that is rooted deep in the person and Word of Christ? Take a moment to write out in your own words what you believe about this beatitude.

Chapter Three

The Meek

*"Blessed are the meek:
for they shall inherit the earth."*
~ Matthew 5:5

The world teaches us that meek is weak. They say it with disdain and we hear sayings like, "She was meek as a mouse." However, the biblical word meek does not mean weakness, but rather strength brought under control. Another word for meekness is gentleness, and I loved the way Elisa Morgan defined gentleness in her book, "Naked Fruit." She defined it as a harnessed power or a bent will. George A. Edgar said it this way, *"Meekness is really the power of self-control."* [3]

To be meek isn't to be weak—quite to the contrary—to be meek is to be strong enough to hold back when you know you have the power to move forward. Meek and weak might rhyme, but that's about as far as their similarities go.

In Matthew 11:28-30 Jesus said, *"Come unto me, all ye that labour and are heavy laden, and I will give you rest.*

Take my yoke upon you, and learn of me; for I am meek and lowly in heart: and ye shall find rest unto your souls. For my yoke is easy, and my burden is light" (KJV). Did you know Jesus was meek?

In "Meekness: The Humble Fruit and Harvest of Confidence," Gina Rodriguez wrote, *"Yes, Jesus was meek and humble. Yet, He was the strongest of the strong, the bravest of the brave."*[4] I love the picture that paints of meekness.

In the introduction I said I learned early on in this study that the beatitudes are not multiple choice. They are characteristics we have as reflections of our Savior. All Christians are meek—even if we cover it with our pride and sinful nature. It's part of becoming Christ-like. When we accept Jesus as our Savior, God plants meekness in our hearts—He grows it in our souls.

So what does meekness look like in our lives? I like to think of meekness as the ability to hold my tongue when I'd rather give someone a piece of my mind. But true meekness goes much deeper. I can't imagine that Christ walked around wanting to lecture everyone He saw (knowing their hearts I'm sure He would have had a good reason to). No, meekness stems from the heart. It's not about knowing you have the power to hurt someone and holding back, it's more about loving God and wanting to share His greatness with the world—to further the kingdom of God with our lives.

When we truly submit to God, we let Him determine our actions and reactions. Meekness stems from our love for God and a desire to share Him with others. It's not so much about holding back as it is about choosing how to move forward in a way that glorifies Him.

Even when we fail to do that, we know Christ's meekness has been credited to us through faith. We all sin and fall short the glory of God (Romans 3:23), but Jesus died so we could be forgiven. God sent the Holy Spirit to live inside of us and transform us to be like Christ. Which means we can claim the promise of Christ that we will inherit the earth. It's God's gift to us—a blessing from above. It's not a choice we make or something we can earn. When we surrender to Christ, He welcomes us with open arms into His Kingdom, both now and forever more.

> *"But the meek shall inherit the land,*
> *And shall delight themselves in the abundance of peace."*
> ~ Psalm 37:11

In Other Words...

- ❖ What does it mean to be meek and where does it come from? (Psalm 149:4; Galatians 5:22-23; 1 Peter 3:3-4; Matthew 11:28-30; Colossians 1:11-14)

- ❖ What did Jesus mean when He said the meek would "inherit the earth"? (1 Peter 1:3-7; Matthew 25:31-34; 2 Peter 3:13; Revelation 21:1-4)

- ❖ Do I have a superficial "Pharisee" faith about meekness, or a real, Christ-like faith rooted deeply in the person and Word of Christ? Take a moment to write, in your own words, what you believe about this beatitude.

Chapter Four

Hunger and Thirst

" Blessed are they that hunger and thirst after righteousness: for they shall be filled."
~ Matthew 5:6

I have quite the sweet tooth. My friends all got a kick out of it the day I posted a Facebook status that said, "Help! I'm craving chocolate and have lost my M&Ms!" I scoured the whole house up and down to find my giant bag of M&Ms that I keep hidden from my children (I do share on occasion—really, I do).

I'm sure you'll be relieved to hear I found them and my craving was fulfilled, but what's even better is the way God has used that craving to draw me close to Him. It all started with a question, "When was the last time I craved God enough to search Him out?"

We crave a lot of things: chocolate, steak, a good book. But how often do we crave God or His Word? That's what the words Jesus spoke in Matthew 5:6 make me wonder. Do

I really hunger and thirst for righteousness? What would that even look (or feel) like?

And those questions led me to the apostle Paul. I think Paul really understood this. He wrote to the Philippians, *"I long to know Christ and the power which is in His resurrection, and to share in His sufferings and die even as He died; in the hope that I may attain to the resurrection from among the dead"* (3:10-11 WNT).

Paul craved the righteousness by hungering for more of Christ. Earlier in that paragraph he said he counted everything else as a loss. He knew he didn't have any righteousness of his own, but only what he received by faith in Christ (vs. 7-9).

The knowledge of Christ is there for the taking. His life, death, and resurrection are all recorded in the Bible, all we have to do is open it with the intention of learning more about Him. We can't deepen our knowledge of Christ when we open God's Word thinking we already know everything it has to say. We have to be open for God to communicate with us. We have to want to know Him more—to crave Him.

I loved the way one of the women in my Bible study worded this. She said, *"God is a gentleman. He waits for us to come to Him."* A.W. Tozer said it this way, *"God waits to be wanted."* He doesn't demand that we sit and eat. He doesn't stand over us and tell us we can't start our day until we have spent at least half an hour reading His Word and drinking in His Spirit. He waits patiently until we crave Him, and then He fills us to the full.

When we draw close to God, He fills us with peace, hope, love, joy, and so much more. Paul wrote in the book of Romans that he wanted God to fill them with joy and peace so they could overflow with hope (15:13). When we crave God, He does just that. He blesses us with more of Him so we can live life to the fullest (John 10:10).

"It is written, 'Man shall not live by bread alone, but by every word that proceeds out of the mouth of God.'"
~ Matthew 4:4 (WEB)

In Other Words...

- ❖ How would you define righteousness and where would you say it comes from? (2 Corinthians 5:21; Romans 3:21-24; Galatians 5:4-6; Psalm 111:2-3)

- ❖ What does it mean when we hunger and thirst for righteousness? How do we do that? (1 Timothy 6:11; Philippians 3:7-11; 2 Chronicles 15:4)

- ❖ What happens when we are filled with righteousness? (Psalm 40:10; Romans 8:10; Ephesians 4:21-24; John 6:35)

- ❖ Do I have a superficial "Pharisee" faith in this area of my life, or a real Christ-like faith that is rooted deep in the person and Word of Christ? Take a moment to write out in your own words what you believe about craving righteousness.

Chapter Five

Merciful

> *" Blessed are the merciful:*
> *for they shall obtain mercy."*
> *~ Matthew 5:7*

Wonderful, merciful Savior. Precious Redeemer and friend—that's my Jesus. Okay, it's also the first lines of a hymn, [5] but the point is we serve an awesome God, and because of His mercy on us, we have hope. Wikipedia used to have the definition of mercy listed as "the religious term for extending kindness and forgiveness." They have since edited their site to read differently, but I loved that definition. To have mercy means to show compassion. It's holding back just anger and consequences—to lighten or forgo a requirement or punishment.

When we receive mercy we are spared.

The most beautiful example of mercy we will ever know is the mercy God has shown us through the sacrifice of His Son on the cross. We deserve to spend eternity in hell for our sins, but He granted us mercy by providing us a way to spend it with Him instead. It was God's mercy that allowed Him to pour out His grace, transfer His righteous and justifiable anger away from us, and spare us from the eternal consequences of our sin.

In light of that, we are called to show mercy to others. I love the way this is written in the book of Jude. It says, *"But you, beloved, keep building up yourselves on your most holy faith, praying in the Holy Spirit. Keep yourselves in the love of God, looking for the mercy of our Lord Jesus Christ to eternal life. On some have compassion, making a distinction, and some save, snatching them out of the fire with fear, hating even the clothing stained by the flesh"* (1:20-23 WEB).

Being merciful is a combination of acting justly, loving compassion, and walking humbly (Micah 6:8). It can be an attitude or an action—and is usually a combination of the two. It can be as simple as doing the right thing (even when you don't feel like it), or going out of your way to help or forgive someone.

Paul David Tripp and his co-author Timothy S. Lane wrote in their book, "Relationships—A Mess Worth Making," that, *"Mercy does not compromise what is morally right and true."* And they went on to say, *"A commitment to mercy will reveal the treasures of your heart."* [6] I love that last line, but it makes me wonder: Do we treasure God's will? Do we treasure His opinions?

In Luke 6:36 Jesus said, *"be merciful, even as your Father is also merciful" (WEB).* That's what God wants from us. He has been merciful to us beyond reason, and He desires us to be merciful to the rest of His creation—not because we have to, but out of love for Him and thanksgiving for what He has done for us.

Merciful

The blessing of being merciful is being transformed to be more like Christ. It's being filled with His Spirit and being aligned with His will. And that blessing is an act of mercy from God, our Father.

> *"May mercy, peace and love be abundantly granted to you."*
> ~ Jude 1:2 (WNT)

In Other Words...

- ❖ How would you define mercy in your own words? (Micah 6:8; Isaiah 30:18)

- ❖ In what ways has God shown mercy to you? (Proverbs 28:13-14; Titus 3:5; 1 Peter 1:3)

- ❖ How has God called us to show mercy to others—and to whom should we show it? (Luke 10:30-37; Romans 12:1; James 3:13-17; Jude 1:20-23)

- ❖ When it comes to mercy, do I have a superficial "Pharisee" faith or a real, Christ-like faith rooted deeply in the person and Word of Christ? Take a moment to write, in your own words, what you believe about this beatitude.

Chapter Six

Pure in Heart

> *"Blessed are the pure in heart:*
> *for they shall see God."*
> ~ Matthew 5:8

    I volunteer for a teen girl's ministry, and it would be fair to say that purity is somewhat of a hot topic. One of the questions I get the most is: How far is too far? I always have the same answer, but I doubt it's the answer any of them are really seeking. I say that all of us have crossed a line when it comes to purity at one point of time or another.

    You see, purity means "unmixed." As Christians, we could say true purity means to be untainted by sin—it isn't just about relationships between guys and girls. True purity is a matter of the heart, and God doesn't give us a checklist of actions we should and shouldn't do to remain pure. God wants us to love Him as He loves us. And He wants our actions to be a result of that love, not because He drew a line (John 14:23-24).

If you're living your life deeply in love with God, the Holy Spirit will guide you in all of your decision-making. You won't need to ask, "How far is too far?" because you'll know the answer deep within your soul. You'll hear the still small voice telling you what you're doing (or thinking about doing) is wrong.

While we know that we all sin (Romans 3:23), thankfully we also know we are purified through Christ. Hebrews 10:22 says, "*let us draw near with sincerity and unfaltering faith, having had our hearts sprinkled, once for all, from consciences oppressed with sin, and our bodies bathed in pure water*" (WNT) Because of what Jesus did for us, we know that one day we will see God face-to-face.

When I think of seeing God, the first person I think of is Moses and when He saw God on the mountain. In Exodus 3, Moses hid his face because he was afraid to look at God—aren't you thankful we don't have to hide our faces from God? In chapter 33 Moses finally got to see God, but not His face. God hid him in the rock and passed by him, then Moses was allowed just a glimpse of His back. In chapter 44 it says that just speaking with God made Moses' face radiant. Can you imagine how amazing that must have been for Moses!?

Yet, we don't have to wait in wonder about what that will be like. We already know. Paul wrote in the letter to the Romans that God was revealed to us through Christ (1:16-17). And to the Corinthians he wrote that Christ is the very image of God (2 Corinthians 4:4-6). We've already seen a glimpse of God through His Son—our Savior.

I long for the day when I get to see God face-to-face. Because He sent His Son to die for my sins, His Spirit to live in my heart, and He purified my soul, I have complete confidence that day will come. If you've confessed Him as the Lord of your life, it will come for you, too. Until then, His Spirit will be that gentle whisper deep within our souls (1 Kings 19:11-14). We can come into His presence with full assurance that He has our best interests at heart—that's the blessing for the pure in heart.

"This I pray, that your love may abound yet more and more in knowledge and all discernment; so that you may approve the things that are excellent; that you may be sincere and without offense to the day of Christ; being filled with the fruits of righteousness, which are through Jesus Christ, to the glory and praise of God."
~ Philippians 1:9-11 (WEB)

In Other Words...

- ❖ How do our hearts become pure? (1 John 3:2-3; 2 Timothy 2:22; Hebrews 10:22; James 1:27; Philippians 2:14-15; Proverbs 16:2)

- ❖ What was that like when Moses saw God? (Exodus 3:5-6; Exodus 33:19-23; Exodus 34:29-35) How does that compare to the way we see God today? (2 Corinthians 4:4-6; Romans 1:16-17)

- ❖ Do I have a superficial "Pharisee" faith in this area of my life, or a real, Christ-like faith rooted deeply in the person and Word of Christ? Take a moment to write, in your own words, what you believe about this beatitude.

Chapter Seven

Peacemakers

"Blessed are the peacemakers:
for they shall be called sons of God."
~ Matthew 5:9

In John 14, Jesus said, *"Peace I leave with you. My peace I give to you; not as the world gives, give I to you. Don't let your heart be troubled, neither let it be fearful."* (vs. 27 WEB). Have you ever stopped to wonder how the peace of God is different than the peace of the world? The more I think about it, the more different they really appear.

The peace of God comes from doing what's right, and in the world, doing the right thing can cause friction, pain, or consequences. The peace of God isn't dependent on circumstances, while worldly peace is. The peace of God is eternal, while worldly peace is temporary.

What it comes down to is that God is a God of peace, not a God at peace. It isn't just a state of being for Him; it's who He is. And Jesus is our Prince of Peace (Isaiah 9:6).

In his letter to the Colossians Paul wrote about Christ, *"...it was the Father's gracious will that the whole of the divine perfections should dwell in Him. And God purposed through Him to reconcile the universe to Himself, making peace through His blood, which was shed upon the Cross-- to reconcile to Himself through Him, I say, things on earth and things in Heaven"* (1:19-20 WNT). Because of Jesus, we can be at peace with God, and experience the peace of God.

As Christians, we long to become more like Christ, so it should come as no surprise that all throughout the Bible, we are instructed to live in peace. Psalm 34:14 says to turn from evil and seek peace—to pursue it. Hebrews 12:14 tells us to make every effort to live in peace. God wants us to be peaceful as He is peaceful.

I love the words Paul wrote to the Philippians, *"In nothing be anxious, but in everything, by prayer and petition with thanksgiving, let your requests be made known to God. And the peace of God, which surpasses all understanding, will guard your hearts and your thoughts in Christ Jesus."* (4:6-7 WEB). When we truly trust God with everything, He will give us peace deep within our souls.

I've felt that peace on and off through my life, but I remember it the strongest when my youngest son was battling cancer. I knew I had a great God and He carried me through that time. I really did have a peace that surpassed all understanding. But we don't only receive God's peace when tragedy strikes. He can fill us with peace every second of every day if we let Him. But we don't. We try to get through life on our own. We worry. We struggle. We try to do things our own way.

Have you ever read through the "ands" in the Bible? God doesn't just tell us to live at peace, He gives us "ands."

Here are a few examples to show you what I mean (emphasis mine):

Philippians 4:9 – *"The things which you learned, received, heard, and saw in me: **do these things, and the God of peace will be with you.**"* (WEB)

Romans 14:19 – *"let us follow after things which **make for peace, and things by which we may build one another up.**"* (WEB)

Colossians 3:15 – *"**let the peace of God rule in your hearts… and be thankful.**"* (WEB)

Romans 8:6 – *"to be carnally minded is death; but **to be spiritually minded is life and peace.**"* (KJV)

The key to true peace is trust in God. It's obeying His commands and living to please Him. When we trust and obey, He fills us with the peace that surpasses all understanding and we are able to inspire peace in others wherever we go. And, as Jesus reminded us in the beatitudes, peacemakers are the children of God. *"For as many as are led by the Spirit of God, these are sons of God."* (Romans 8:14).

Before we can become peacemakers, we must first come to know the God of peace. We have to have peace before we can make it. But when we are blessed with God-given peace deep within us, we don't go around stirring up trouble, but encouraging, building up, and making peace—we become peacemakers.

"The Lord bless thee, and keep thee: The Lord make his face shine upon thee, and be gracious unto thee: The Lord lift up his countenance upon thee, and give thee peace."
~ Numbers 6:24-26 (KJV)

In Other Words...

- ❖ How does God's peace differ from that of the world's? (Ezekiel 37:26a; John 14:27)

- ❖ Are you pursuing a life of peace? If not, what changes do you need to make? (Hebrews 12:11; Job 22:21; Philippians 4:7-9)

- ❖ How have you seen God's peace in you inspire peace in others? (Proverbs 15:1; Titus 3:1-2)

- ❖ Do I have a superficial "Pharisee" faith in this area of my life, or a real, Christ-like faith rooted deeply in the person and Word of Christ? Take a moment to write, in your own words, what you believe about this beatitude.

Chapter Eight

Persecuted

"Blessed are they that have been persecuted for righteousness' sake: for theirs is the kingdom of heaven."
~ Matthew 5:10

Mary* was my best friend growing up. We went everywhere and did everything together, and one summer that led to the biggest change in my life. It was the summer after our eighth grade year, and Mary invited me to go to church camp with her. I had been going to various church camps ever since I could walk, but this one was different. The speaker told us that God wanted to have a personal relationship with us.

I was blown away.

Prior to this, I knew God as a fact of life. He'd always been there. He created everything. But I never knew you could actually have a one-on-one relationship with Him. That week I gave my life to Christ. And Mary thought it was cool. She and her dad invited me to start attending church with them. So I did.

As our high school years flew by, I noticed Mary and I were starting to drift a bit. I made other friends at church, and she seemed to distance herself a bit. After we graduated, and our other friends moved on, we ended up getting an apartment together. That's when it happened.

It turns out I had missed the fact that my best friend didn't have a personal relationship with Jesus. I knew she wasn't on fire for Christ like I was, but I hadn't grasped that she was fed up with all the "Jesus stuff." Apparently my "holier-than-thou" attitude was the last straw. The girl that played such a huge part in leading me to Christ walked out of my life because of my love for Him.

I'm still friends with Mary's family, but Mary herself won't talk to me. Even after all these years that still hurts. In chapter two we talked about mourning, I mourn for the loss of our friendship, and I mourn for her soul.

That's just one of many ways we can suffer persecution as Christians. For me, it came from my best friend. For you it might be a son or daughter, a father or mother, an aunt, a cousin, a friend, a coworker, or a neighbor. Christians face persecution from multiple sources, in multiple different ways, and on multiple different levels.

But, it just so happens, God is prepared for that.

The Bible talks about persecution quite a bit. Jesus spoke about it as a fact of life (and it is). In Matthew 10 (16-22) Jesus said He was sending us out like sheep among wolves.

Persecution doesn't always come in the form of government's imprisoning, beating, or killing Christians (though all of those do still happen today—find out more at: https://www.persecution.com/). Persecution can come from friends and family disowning us because of Christ (Mark

Persecuted

10:29-31). It can come from people in the work place treating us unfairly. It can even come from other Christians.

Paul often wrote of persecution and troubles as a way to deepen our faith. In the parable of the sowers, it was discussed as a way to test our faith. Jesus said, *"In the same way those who receive the seed on the rocky places are those who, when they have heard the Message, at once accept it joyfully, but they have no root within them. They last for a time; then, when suffering or persecution comes because of the Message, they are immediately overthrown."* (Mark 4:16-17 WNT). In order to endure persecution, we have to be rooted in our faith. And those roots stem from love.

We are charged in James chapter 1 to count it as joy when we face trials (vs. 2-3). We can do that because of love. We can rejoice when we are persecuted, not because of the pain, but because we love God and are willing to do what He wants no matter what the cost. After all, He sent His Son to die on the cross for our sins, and to grant us entry into the kingdom of heaven out of love for us. If we truly love Him, we should be willing to stand up for Him when the stakes are far less.

As I close this chapter, I invite you to pray for those who persecute you (Matthew 5:44). I still pray for Mary. I think of her often and long for her to come to really know what a glorious savior we have in Christ. I don't know who is persecuting you, but I do encourage you to pray for them.

I also want to encourage you. Facing persecution of any kind isn't easy, but God knows what you are going through. Spending eternity with Him, receiving the kingdom of heaven, that's worth the heartache we face on earth. Give your sorrow to Him, and He will give you refuge and comfort. And what a blessing that is.

Blessings from Above

"We are hard pressed, yet never in absolute distress;
perplexed, yet never utterly baffled;
pursued, yet never left unsuccoured;
struck to the ground, yet never slain;
always, wherever we go,
carrying with us in our bodies the putting to death of Jesus,
so that in our bodies it may also be clearly shown
that Jesus lives."

~ 2 Corinthians 4:8-10 (WNT)

In Other Words...

- ❖ Has anyone ever looked down on you or persecuted you because you were a Christian? What was that like and what was your reaction? (James 1:2-4; Romans 5:1-5; 2 Corinthians 12:10)

- ❖ How does God want you to react when people mistreat you because of your faith? (Matthew 5:43-48)

- ❖ Do I have a superficial "Pharisee" faith in this area of my life, or a real, Christ-like faith rooted deeply in the person and Word of Christ? Take a moment to write, in your own words, what you believe about this beatitude. (Galatians 2:20; 1 Corinthians 13:13; John 13:34-35)

* Name has been changed to protect privacy.

Conclusion

"Blessed are you when they have insulted and persecuted you, and have said every cruel thing about you falsely for my sake. Be joyful and triumphant, because your reward is great in the Heavens; for so were the Prophets before you persecuted."
~ Matthew 5:11-12 (WNT)

We have officially came full circle, and I don't think that was a coincidence on Jesus' part. The first beatitude was, *"Blessed are the poor in spirit: for theirs is the kingdom of heaven."* Remember when I talked about the church of Philadelphia. They were persecuted, but Jesus comforted them and promised them eternity with Him.

Then He repeated part of that with the last verse saying, *"Blessed are they that have been persecuted for righteousness' sake: for theirs is the kingdom of heaven."* Nothing's changed. Christians will inherit the kingdom of heaven. Life will hurt, but God is good.

The Christian life is one of humility and surrender. Of grieving sin and craving more of God. It's a life of forgiveness and compassion in the face of painful persecution. It's a life of promoting peace and focusing on our Savior. The Christian life is a life full of blessings from above—but not because of what we've done. It's all because of what was done for us.

Life won't always be easy. In fact, Jesus promised us that in this world, we will have trouble (John 16:33). But when we have Christ as our savior, and are able to look at the bigger picture, our outlook on life changes. Circumstances no longer matter. What matters is knowing Christ and making Him known.

Knowing the love of God, our sinful state, and the sacrifice of our Savior is the biggest blessing any of us could ever hope for. So often, we take all of that for granted, and, for me, this study through the beatitudes has been an amazing reminder of how blessed I really am.

If you only take one thing away from this study, I pray it is a deep-seated knowledge of how much you are blessed just by knowing Christ and having Him in your life.

The blessings spoken of in the beatitudes have nothing to do with our physical surroundings or circumstances, but have everything to do with the attitudes of our hearts. They don't speak of earthly blessings, but heavenly ones. These blessings don't tarnish, fade, or come and go; they consist of the peace that surpasses all understanding, eternal life, and the joy of knowing we are loved by the Creator of the world.

Scott Dannemiller wrote an article for the Huffington Post where he summed up the beatitudes perfectly. Here's a short excerpt:

Conclusion

"So my prayer today is that I understand my true blessing. It's not my house. Or my job. Or my standard of living.

No.

My blessing is this. I know a God who gives hope to the hopeless. I know a God who loves the unlovable. I know a God who comforts the sorrowful. And I know a God who has planted this same power within me. Within all of us.

And for this blessing, may our response always be,

'Use me.'"[7]

Let us always be grateful for the things God has given us, while remembering true blessings aren't materialistic. They don't fade. True blessings come from knowing who God is, what He has done, and what He will do. Being blessed isn't a state of being, but a fact. It's a truth nothing can change.

"Blessed is he whose transgression is forgiven, whose sin is covered. Blessed is the man unto whom the Lord imputeth not iniquity, and in whose spirit there is no guile."
~ Psalm 32:1-2 (KJV)

In Other Words...

- ❖ Does my faith in Christ affect the way I look at life? Why or why not? (Romans 12:2; Romans 6:1-14; Ephesians 4:17-32)

- ❖ How are you blessed by knowing Christ and having Him in your life?

- ❖ When it comes to true blessings, do I have a superficial "Pharisee" faith, or a real, Christ-like faith rooted deeply in the person and Word of Christ? Take a moment to write what you've learned about the beatitudes during this study.

- ❖ Optional: Has God shown you anything new during this study? Has it impacted your life at all? I would love to hear from you! Would you consider leaving an honest review on Amazon and sharing some of the things God has shown you through this study? I read through all my reviews and love hearing from readers. Reviews help other readers, too. If you'd consider doing that, you can leave a review at: http://www.amazon.com/dp/B00JAN7DT4/

  You can also contact me directly by visiting: http://www.paulandheatherhart.com/contact/

Sources

1 Barclay, William. The Gospel of Matthew. V.1 (Chapters 1 to 10) Revised Edition. Trans, by William Barclay. Philadelphia: The Westminster Press, 1958.

2. Laura Story Music. Laura Story - "Blessings" Story Behind The Song. Feb 15, 2011. YouTube. http://youtu.be/gjB2skJi2co (March 2014).

3. Morgan, Elisa. Naked Fruit. Grand Rapids, MI. Fleming H. Revell, 2004.

4. Rodriguez, Gina. Meekness: The Humble Fruit and Harvest of Confidence. Gina Rodriguez, 2013.

5. Rodgers, Dawn and Wyse, Eric. Lyrics. Wonderful, Merciful Savior. The copyright for "Wonderful, Merciful Savior" is owned and controlled by Word Music, LLC © 1989 Word Music ASCAP/ Dayspring Music BMI. http://www.wonderfulmercifulsavior.com (September, 26 2014).

6. Lane, Timothy S. and Tripp, Paul David. Relationships: A Mess Worth Making. New Growth Press, 2006.

7. Dannemiller, Scott. The One Thing Christians Should Stop Saying. The Huffington Post, February, 27 2014. http://www.huffingtonpost.com/scott-dannemiller/christians -should-stop-saying_b_4868963.html (March 2014).

Free Discussion Guides

Would you be interested in studying the beatitudes with your small group? It is one of several Bible studies available free from www.paulandheatherhart.com.

Study Guides in this Series:

Beatitudes
(Matthew 5:3-12)

Fruit of the Spirit
(Galatians 5:22-23)

Armor of God
(Ephesians 6:10-20)

Letters to the Churches
(Revelation 1-3)

Find a complete list of study guides at:
http://www.paulandheatherhart.com/bible-study/

About the Author

Heather Hart is first and foremost a servant of Christ who is happily married to the man of her dreams - but she's also a book marketing expert, internationally best-selling author, and the manager of multiple websites including, BooklyBooks and TrainingAuthors.com. She has been writing devotions for FindYourTrueBeauty.com since 2009. With her husband, Paul, she helped found their brother ministry FindYourTrueStrength.com for teen guys in 2013.

Heather also writes Bible studies (like this one) for her local church and enjoys working from home where she spends her days studying God's Word, typing on her computer, and encouraging those around her. When she's not writing or absorbed in her four children, Heather can usually be found with her nose in a book.

Find out more by visiting:
www.PaulandHeatherHart.com

More Books with Heather Hart

Teen Devotionals… for Girls!

Teen Devotionals… for Girls! Volume 2

21 Teen Devotionals… for Girls!

21 Prayers for Teen Girls

21 Stories of Gratitude

Unshackled and Free

Body Image Lies Women Believe

See a complete list of Heather's Books at:
http://www.paulandheatherhart.com/heather/

Author's Note

"For where two or three are gathered together in my name, there am I in the midst of them."
~ Matthew 18:20

More than anything else, relationships with other Christian women have helped me grow in my walk with God. Don't tune out—I'm not being heretical, I promise.

When Christian women come together, God is there (Matthew 18:20). He can do amazing things when we are in groups!

In my own life, I've seen this time and time again. When my twins were born, I had four children all five and under—I might not have survived that first year without the women God brought to me. I felt alone and isolated. My husband was working 12-14 hour shifts six days a week at that point and I didn't feel like I could go anywhere—and didn't know anyone anyway. During that time, God used an online community of Christian moms, and even what I would call mentorship through Nancy Leigh DeMoss and her online ministry Revive Our Hearts, to draw me closer to Him and give me the strength to keep breathing.

Later on, God opened the doors to start attending a women's Bible study at my church. We met together weekly, studied God's Word, and supported one another. It was awesome.

Proverbs 27:17 says that iron sharpens iron—and I believe Christian women do that for each other. In Hebrews 10:25 we are encouraged to meet together and encourage one another (see also Hebrews 3:13), and we are called to confess our sins to each other in James 5:16.

Titus 2:3-5 says older women are supposed to learn to be Christians, and then teach younger women to follow suit. Yes, that is simplified and paraphrased, but it's the basics. I know I may not be older than you, and you may be more mature in your faith than I am, but I know we all can learn from each other. Even when I've discipled women younger than me, it's never been one-sided. God uses us to sharpen one another.

While I know any fellowship between Christian women is beneficial, what I love the most is coming together to study God's Word. 2 Timothy 3:16-17 (WEB) says:

"Every Scripture is God-breathed and profitable for teaching, for reproof, for correction, and for instruction in righteousness, that the man of God may be complete, thoroughly equipped for every good work."

Equipped for every good work. That includes the good work of motherhood—or grand parenting. It includes the good work of being a wife, daughter, friend, servant of Christ, employee, manager, whatever "work" you do. If it's honorable, then the Bible was written to help equip you for it.

Studying God's Word with other women provides fellowship to help you apply it to your life. In my own case, it provides some much needed accountability. Accountability to keep pushing forward, when it would be easier to give up. Accountability to apply what I'm learning and live it out. Accountability to live a life worthy of the calling God has given me (Eph. 4:1).

Do you need that accountability in your walk with God? Would you benefit from fellowship with other Christian women?

I can't think of a single time in my life where I wasn't thankful for or praying for fellowship with women just like you. I might not know you personally, and I don't know where you are in your walk with God, but I do know God brought you to this book for a reason. I strongly encourage you to get plugged in with a group of women in your own community, if you aren't already.

Whether we realize it or not, we all need each other. Every Christian woman can be a blessing to another Christian woman. I want to close this book with words found in 2 John (vs. 5-6 WEB):

"Now I beg you, dear lady,
not as though I wrote to you a new commandment,
but that which we had from the beginning, that we love one another. This is love, that we should walk according to his commandments. This is the commandment,
even as you heard from the beginning,
that you should walk in it."

Acknowledgements

First and foremost, I must give thanks to the Lord of my life, Jesus Christ. To Him be the glory and honor and praises. He has taught me so much, and I am eternally grateful. Without Him, this book would have never come to be.

Beverly Kinnibrugh has been a huge inspiration to me. She organized our Monday morning ladies' Bible study and encouraged me to take our study and publish it as a book. Her encouragement, support, and friendship means more to me than she will ever know.

I'd also like to thank each and every one of the ladies that attend our weekly Bible studies. Each one of you is a joy and your faithfulness is such a blessing to me.

Nell, Dana, Ruth, Jeanie, Beverly, and Barbra one and Barbra two, I treasure the wisdom and insight you share each week. You are all wonderful examples of Titus 2 women. Thank you for pouring into me and everyone else who attends our studies.

Of course, I'd like to thank the local First Baptist Church for allowing us to meet each week and feeding us lunch. Deidra has been amazing to print our study sheets and do all the other behind-the-scenes work. We all are forever thankful for Scotty who lets us in and turns on the heat.

Special thanks to Shelley Hitz. She has been a constant encouragement in my publishing journey and has acted as a sounding board on more than one occasion. Without the knowledge Shelley has shared with me, I never would have been able to publish this book.

I'm extremely thankful for the love and support of my husband, Paul, who I like to refer to as Mr. Amazing—because, he is the most amazing man I've ever had the privilege of meeting. My love for him grows stronger every single day and I'm so thankful God brought him into my life. He has helped me with my book covers, acted as a sounding board, and encouraged me every step of the way.

Last, but not least, thank you, dear reader, for taking the time to read to the very last page. I'm thankful for you as well. I pray God blesses you with a wonderful group of friends and family, just as He has done for me.